# Doug Osborne
# DOES NOT QUIT

## The House Behind My Banner

D1519455

## Doug Osborne

ISBN-13: 9798388938732

# DEDICATION

To everyone who has believed in me and supported me on my mission.

NOT TODAY!

# Contents

# Introduction

My first house has been everything I needed to pursue and soon achieve my goals. Buying it was far from easy, but I did not quit and the day I closed on this house was the best of my life so far.

This is the story of the start of my mission of getting a job and going off disability, and of the battle to buy my first house so I could continue my mission. The period between March 18th, 2021, when I applied for jobs for the first time in over seven years, and August 6th, 2021, when I closed on the purchase of this house, was by far the most stressful of my life. That includes the ten months I've been interviewing for jobs since I hung my banner. Because in 2021, I was fighting to overcome my disability and to avoid becoming disabled again.

# Part 1

# The Mission and the House

The start of my mission, how it was delayed by my landlord's plan to sell his property, and my plan to buy my first house so I could resume my mission.

# The Start of My Mission

Hi, my name is on my banner. I'm a software engineer who once had a successful career, but I became depressed after moving to Chicago at the end of 2013. As a result of this depression, I haven't been employed since 2016 and have been on Social Security Disability Insurance since 2018.

Although it is primarily the depression that made me disabled, I am also diagnosed with autism spectrum disorder and ADHD. Consequently, I have found that my environment has been a major factor in my level of functioning. I have been thriving since I bought my first house in 2021, but I was a shell of myself between 2016 and 2018 when I lived in small apartments with lots of distractions.

So in 2019, I rented a house in northwest Connecticut, which was a much better environment for me to write software.

The house I rented in CT.

My office at the house in CT.

I liked living in this house for the most part. The main exception was that my landlord, "Bob," sometimes bullied me and made my life more stressful, even before the events described here.

When I went on disability, my original plan was to pursue my own unique software projects, with the idea that eventually one of them would lead to my success again. While I'm proud of these projects shown on my portfolio, the end of 2020 was a low point for me because they hadn't led to anything yet and I was running out of motivation to write software on my own. I was also running out of money because the house in Connecticut cost more than I could afford on disability. This was a calculated risk because my previous two apartments were poor environments for me where I didn't have a chance to overcome my disability.

At the start of 2021, I began my mission of getting a work-from-home job and going off disability. Shortly afterward, Bob told me he was interested in selling the house I was renting. I told him that I was interested in buying his house, but that I needed to get a job first to afford it. I wasn't aware of his urgency to sell his house until after I started applying for jobs.

I was feeling rather disabled in December 2020 because my depression had reached another peak and I was becoming less and less productive. To start digging myself out of this hole, my focus in January 2021 was on self-discipline and productivity. After working hard to restore some of my self-confidence, I began preparing to apply for jobs in February by documenting my software projects at doug-osborne.com.

# The Dream Job

On Thursday, March 18th, 2021, I submitted my first job applications in over seven years. The next day, Bob asked me via a text message if I was still interested in buying his house. I told him that I was, but that I had just started applying for jobs and couldn't give a definitive answer until I got one. Bob then sent me the following message.

> Ok Doug you need to let me know by March 30 and if you are buying I will need a deposit by April 15 if not you will need to vacate by the 15 of April so I can clean up and list it for May 1 let me know as soon as possible. Thank you.

To summarize, Bob just told me that I had to either buy his house or get off his property in less than one month. If interviewing for jobs while on disability wasn't hard enough, suddenly my housing situation made it ten times as stressful.

I knew that Bob was being unrealistic by giving me less than a month to vacate, especially with COVID-related eviction moratoriums still in place. Later, I received a signed letter from Bob that adjusted the move out date to April 30th, although I knew I had more time before Bob could legally force me off his property. Still, the clock was now ticking, and I felt like my options were:

1. Get a job so I could possibly buy Bob's house. Getting a job would also open a lot of other options.
2. Find another suitable environment for me to live and work productively, a challenge given my income and autism/ADHD.
3. Give up on my mission.

Having just applied for jobs, I initially pursued the ideal outcome of getting a job first. Due to my very first application since 2013, on Tuesday, March 23rd, I was invited to begin the interview process for a possible dream job: A Senior Software Engineer position that paid five times my disability income, at a company rated more highly to work for than Google and Facebook.

I gave it my best shot and despite feeling enormous pressure, I passed a phone screen, a software engineering assessment, and another interview to reach the penultimate interview on April 13th. Sadly, on April 15th, I found out that I didn't make it to the final interview. I still believe I would have gotten that job if not for the stress caused by my unstable housing situation. Unfortunately, getting that job would have also made resolving this situation a whole lot easier.

# Postponing My Mission

I was hoping to continue my job search while renting Bob's house, but after receiving possibly my most painful rejection letter on April 15th, it was clear that I could no longer hope that a job would resolve my housing situation. I then wrote a letter to Bob, in which I shared an update and tried to start negotiating for a mutually beneficial agreement.

When Bob didn't respond to my letter or follow-up text message, I decided to postpone my job search to find another place to live. It would be nearly a year before my next job application.

I first looked for other places that I could rent, but I couldn't find any suitable places for me to work from home that I could afford on disability. My mother tried to help and found a stand-alone condo for sale that she liked at a complex we used to live at. Our idea was to buy it together, then I would live there until I got a job and could buy my own place, and then she would move in and eventually retire there. Unfortunately, we couldn't get approved for a mortgage together. However, due to my mother's efforts, I was pre-approved for a mortgage for a home purchase of up to $150,000 on Tuesday, May 4th.

Also on May 4th, Bob finally responded to my letter and follow-up text message.

```
Hi Doug after much considera-
tion I have decided to turn
this over to my attorney I
made my intentions clear in my
last letter . You have chosen
```

```
to ignore me along with the
yard and your dog destroying
my property I think it's best
that she handles it from here.
Communication   from   now   on
will be through her she will
be in touch.
```

Bob, who had called me a "great tenant" less than six months ago, seemed to be exaggerating just a bit. For example, here is a picture of the yard he claimed I was ignoring, taken on that same day, along with a picture of the beast that somehow managed to "destroy" his property.

Bob's property on 5/4/21.

The dog that "destroyed" Bob's property.

In my opinion, Bob's unrealistic demands had potentially cost me my dream job. Meanwhile, I was doing him a big favor by postponing my job search to find another place to live so he could sell his house. I talked to a friend of mine who was a landlord, and he advised me to ignore Bob and continue applying for jobs. Later, I talked to real estate agents who complained that they couldn't sell houses because the tenants refused to leave.

I wasn't sure what Bob expected his attorney to do given that CT's eviction moratorium made it illegal for him to kick me out back then. Yet, I wasn't feeling safe while living at his property, especially after hearing stories about Bob's spitefulness and how he had made previous tenants' lives miserable while pursuing "revenge."

After I got pre-approved for a mortgage, I decided to buy my first house. On Friday, May 7th, I sent Bob another letter informing him of my intentions and offering full cooperation with his plans to sell his property during my house search. Regrettably, Bob ignored my letter, and he wasn't done getting in the way of my life's plans.

# The Dream House

Getting pre-approved for a mortgage wasn't enough for me to buy a house because I needed help with the down payment and closing costs. My mother wasn't able to help me, and I found out my father wasn't either after I sent him a five-page email on May 11th. Two days later, I was very lucky to receive an offer to help from my uncle and mother's brother, who was and still is battling bladder cancer.

Unfortunately, the inflated housing market that made Bob want to sell his property also made it difficult for me to find a house I liked and could afford on disability. I would have preferred staying close to my family, but there was practically nothing in my price range in CT. So, I extended my search north up to Vermont and west to Central NY State. I had always wanted to live out in a cabin in the woods somewhere, so I was mainly looking at houses in remote areas. I flagged about forty properties on Zillow, but there was one that stood out above the rest.

On Saturday, May 15th, I took a two-and-a-half-hour drive to look at my first and only house during my search, a four-season vacation home in Summit, NY.

The outside of the house I bought in Summit, NY.

The inside of the house I bought in Summit, NY.

I fell in love with the house immediately. It wasn't quite the "remote cabin in the woods," but it felt like one from the inside, especially when looking out back. It also came with deeded lake access, which I've used to train for my goal of competing in triathlons again.

A panorama shot from my lake access, taken on 8/22/21.

I made an offer to buy the house the next day, May 16th. I agreed to terms with the sellers on Saturday, May 22nd, and was thrilled to get the house for below the asking price, with a lot of nice furniture included. I was so excited that I drove out there again to show it to my mother on May 23rd. At the time, I had little idea of how long it would take to complete the purchase of my first house.

On Saturday, May 29th, I took a third trip to see the property for an inspection. My inspector was very thorough and found a lot of minor issues, but nothing major, so I was fine with it. It took some convincing to get my uncle's approval though, which I needed because he is an investor in my property. There was another inspection and appraisal on Wednesday, June 2nd, which were required for my FHA loan. The sellers remedied the two minor problems with the FHA inspection by June 8th. After considerable sweating, I finally received a loan commitment letter from my lender on Thursday, June 15th, which I signed immediately.

I had been told that the loan commitment is when a home purchase goes from "if" to "when." So, starting on June 15th, I enjoyed a brief respite from the overwhelming stress I had felt since March 18th. There was another little strain involving the gift funds I needed to close on my house purchase, but this was relieved when I received these funds on Monday, June 21st.

Two months after receiving that painful rejection letter, I finally felt like I was going to get another shot to complete my mission, and from an even better environment than my home in Connecticut.

# Part 2

# The Eviction

The eviction lawsuit that violated Connecticut's eviction moratorium and jeopardized my house purchase.

# Get Off My Property

While I was cooperating with his plans of selling his house, Bob wasn't cooperating with my plans to buy my house so I could vacate his property and resume my mission. On Friday, May 27th, I was served the following Notice to Quit Possession by a state marshal.

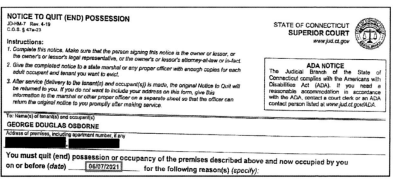

The top portion of the Notice to Quit that I was served on 5/27/21.

This Notice to Quit was signed by Bob's attorney, which surprised me because I thought CT's eviction moratorium protected me from being evicted. Later, I found out that the Notice to Quit violated CT's moratorium. Even then, I knew that while it stated that I must vacate by June 7th, there were still more steps to take before I could be forcibly removed from Bob's property.

To be fair, Bob was unaware that I was in the process of buying a house at that time. I wanted to be more certain about my house purchase before I told Bob, but I took this Notice to Quit as a reminder that Bob really wanted me to get off his property. I also really wanted to move out so I could resume my mission. To show my cooperation and to respect the date on Bob's Notice to Quit, I sent Bob the following text message on Tuesday, June 7th.

> Hi Bob: I bought a house and should be moving out sometime in July.

I chose optimistic wording because I didn't want Bob to stress over the details I was working out to complete my purchase. While Bob didn't respond, I assumed this text message would satisfy him and be the end of his eviction threats. All I had to do was to finish buying my house, and I thought I was in the clear after I signed the loan commitment on June 15th and received the gift funds on June 21st.

# Why Is This Eviction Still Happening?

After receiving the gift funds to close on my house purchase, I only experienced about an hour of relief before I was shocked to see the same state marshal at my home again. I was served a summons to court in a summary process (eviction) action signed by Bob's attorney, "Jill."

A portion of the eviction summons I was served on 6/21/21.

While I felt I could basically ignore the Notice to Quit and only responded to it out of respect, I was now summoned to court and had to do something about it. If I didn't, then the next time I saw a state marshal, they might be forcing me out of my home and onto the street. Furthermore, there was now a public court record of an eviction lawsuit against me. I was worried my lender would find out and change their mind about lending to me, which became an unintentionally self-fulfilling prophecy.

Later, I found out that the summons and attached eviction complaint violated CT's eviction moratorium. At the time, I was almost 100 percent certain that the moratorium would protect me, but I assumed that Bob and his attorney weren't violating any laws and that it was the tenant's responsibility to use it as a defense. However, I tried but couldn't find any instructions online about how to use the moratorium as a defense.

I decided to try representing myself by emailing Jill. In this email, I tried to appeal to Jill's sense of humanity, to demonstrate that I was moving out as quickly as possible, and to subtly point out that continuing to threaten me might not be the best idea. I didn't mention the moratorium because I didn't think I had to recite any laws to an attorney. This is the first sentence of my email, which I sent on Tuesday, June 22nd.

> *Hi Jill: My name is Doug Osborne and I'm a software engineer on disability, diagnosed with autism, ADHD, anxiety and depression.*

After my introduction, I summarized the events since March 18th, and then concluded my email with the following.

> *Since we last spoke on 4/18/21, Bob has refused to talk to me when I couldn't accommodate his unrealistic demand to buy his property or vacate the premises in less than 4 weeks. I had already applied for jobs so I could buy his house, and it was impossible for me to pursue both options at once. Bob has continued to threaten me since, causing my mother and I extreme emotional distress while he carries out this eviction and refuses to show any willingness to compromise. I believe this emotional distress cost me a 150K/year job that would have quadrupled my income.*

*My uncle is helping me buy my first house and is also an investor in the property. He also has to go in for his 4th surgery for bladder cancer tomorrow. I'm obligated to tell my uncle about this eviction because it might cause him to lose his investment, which is part of his estate plans. However, I don't understand why this eviction is happening since I'm doing exactly what Bob wanted and moving out of here as soon as possible.*

*Could you please explain why I'm still being evicted so I can relay that information to my uncle?*

My email was completely true, though I didn't expect to have to tell my uncle about this eviction. I was trying to make the point that Jill's client had already caused my family enough trouble and that it's not just me that Bob is threatening now. I had similar reasons for my introduction, like "why are you picking on a poor guy on disability who is trying to get a job?"

# Pay Up and We'll Talk

I was not expecting Bob and his attorney to seemingly try to take advantage of me with this response to my email, sent on June 23rd.

*Good morning –*

*Thank you for your communication. Mr. Bob started the eviction because the rent hadn't been paid for May and June. Mr. Bob states that if the rent is paid for May, June and July he will negotiate with you. If you purchase your house and move out in July, he would give you back the pro rata share of the rent. (So, for example, if you are out on July 15th, he would give you back the rent for the last ½ of the month.)*

*This is an attempt to collect a debt and any information obtained will be used for that purpose.*

I was very upset by Bob and Jill's response because it felt like they insulted my intelligence and were trying to take advantage of the first sentence of my email. Their answer to my question merely tacked on an extra month to the eviction complaint, which was for a single month of rent due in May. That complaint clearly violated CT's moratorium, which had an exception for nonpayment of at least six months' rent.

Jill didn't even answer my question because I was asking her why she was signing her name on these eviction papers. I already knew the real reason Bob kept threatening me with this eviction: he's a bully, and I pissed him off because I couldn't meet his unrealistic demands. Back in May, Bob chose to bully me with these legal threats, instead of talking to me like a normal person.

Officially, I don't remember whether I sent Bob a check for May because it was an enormously stressful period, and I was forgetting a lot of things. For example, I forgot to send Bob a check in April of 2021, but I sent it as soon as he reminded me via text message on April 3rd.

```
Hey  Doug  haven't  received
your   check  you're  always
early  so  I'm  hoping  it's  not
lost give me a call thank you

Hi  Bob:  sorry  I  have  a  lot
going  on  and  forgot  to  mail
the  check,  I  will  mail  it
shortly.
```

The only time I heard from Bob in May was on the 4th, when he sent his text message that threatened legal action but didn't mention anything about rent.

I asked my landlord friend for his opinion about Jill's response to my email. He said it showed they thought they could intimidate me, and they didn't offer to drop the eviction because they wanted me to remain distressed. In summary, they wanted me to pay them money before they would negotiate the illegal eviction lawsuit.

At the time, I needed every penny I had to close on my first house purchase so I could move out of Bob's property. I thought this was Bob's main concern because he wanted to sell his property while the market was at a record high. Bob's actions actually delayed this, but I eventually moved out and Bob sold his house for over two hundred times the amount on the eviction complaint.

# She Should Have Known Better

I spent some time writing a response to Jill's e-mail, in which I mentioned CT's eviction moratorium, and asked her: "Is this really what you want me to tell my uncle as he's recovering from surgery?" Her email was so offensive that I didn't send that response and decided to talk to another attorney instead.

I tried to reach an eviction attorney that represents tenants, but I hadn't gotten through to any by Friday, June 25th. So, I called a local firm and left a message for their eviction attorney, "Sam", who I suspected was typically on the other side of the aisle.

Sam returned my call on the same day. I told him about my case and Sam confirmed that the moratorium should protect me. He also seemed surprised that the eviction had made it this far, so he looked up my case online. He seemed even more surprised when he found it and asked, "Who's the attorney behind this?"

Then he answered himself, "Oh, Jill? Ah, **she should have known better**."

I told Sam, "Yeah, I think they're just trying to intimidate me."

Sam then said, "I made that mistake once on a Notice to Quit, and I got a call from the judge and it was dismissed within a day."

Somehow Jill's mistake on a Notice to Quit in May went unnoticed, and then she repeated it with a more serious action in June. I asked Sam why my case hadn't been dismissed, and he said it was probably sitting under a pile of papers and the judge hadn't seen it yet.

Sam then told me that I could file a motion to dismiss and he walked me through how to write one. Besides the standard requirements, Sam said that I could simply state that "The Notice to Quit **violates the eviction moratorium** and the case should be dismissed."

Sam asked me if I wanted to countersue Bob and his attorney, and I said, "I might, but right now I just want to get off Bob's property and move into my first house."

Sam was friendly during our first conversation, but he didn't seem nearly as happy to talk to me the following week.

# Can I Go On Offense Now?

After talking to Sam, I realized why I couldn't find instructions for using CT's eviction moratorium as a defense: attorneys weren't supposed to sign their name on these papers to begin with, unless they gave a reason that met one of the moratorium's exceptions, which Jill did not. Now that I knew that Bob and Jill had violated a law more than once, I started thinking about possibly turning the tables and switching from defense to offense. Jill's email had offended me enough that I at least wanted to get an attorney's opinion on the situation.

So, I called Sam on Monday, June 28th at 11:44 AM. Sam seemed a lot more stressed than on Friday, and I got the impression that I was the last person he wanted to hear from. First, I asked him if my motion to dismiss looked correct, which I shared with him via a text message.

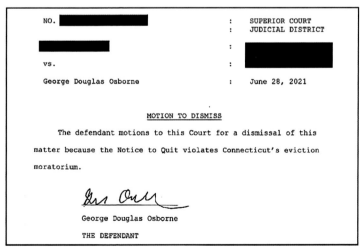

My original motion to dismiss.

Sam thought it was fine then, though he made a few additions to it later. I then told Sam I was thinking about countersuing Jill and Bob. I mentioned my email and how Jill's response had upset me. Sam asked me to share the emails. I told him I wanted to, but in person, because I wasn't comfortable forwarding the email. Sam was very resistant to meeting with me, but I insisted, and we scheduled an in-person appointment for the next day, Tuesday, June 29th at 11 AM.

Sam's demeanor during our call made me suspect that something was already going on regarding my case. I thought Sam had likely been speaking to Jill, and that Jill may have been in some trouble with the judge. I also got the impression that Sam and Jill were friends, and that Sam might have felt like he betrayed Jill by telling me that "she should have known better."

Before our meeting, I was mentally prepared for the possibility that Sam's primary concern would be to protect Jill. Even so, I was hoping Sam would at least provide me with sound legal advice.

# Revenge of the Nerd

My meeting with Sam was the strangest experience I've ever had. I almost wish I recorded it because I was amazed at how I dominated a "legal consultation" with an attorney who had no interest in representing me. Sam only got to recite one law because I saw through his efforts to provoke me and then tell me about other laws I already knew. Conversely, I was able to get about all the information I could from Sam without revealing that I was essentially interrogating him.

I arrived at Sam's firm at 11:01 AM. I was sweaty because it was ninety degrees outside, and I had walked nearly a mile to get there because I didn't have a car. The door was locked, but I called and was let in by the receptionist. I didn't want to sweat on their fancy furniture, so I stood in their waiting room for about five minutes. Then Sam walked in looking very serious and intimidating. Sam, a partner at the firm, was a big, white guy, around sixty with gray hair, and he was wearing a suit. I was wearing cargo shorts and a collared t-shirt, which made it formal attire for me anyway.

As I followed Sam into a conference room, I said, "Nice to meet you, sorry I'm a little sweaty because I walked here."

Sam just kind of choked up, and I don't remember him saying anything in response. This made me think, "wow, this guy is really nervous," a thought reinforced at many points during our meeting.

I sat down, got a folder out of my backpack, and handed Sam a printout of my email and Jill's response. I started to share a backstory and said, "I swear, it felt like they were trying to take advantage of the first sentence of my email."

Sam wasn't interested in my backstory and asked me if he could just read the email. This was the first of several hints that Sam was well-prepared for our meeting and knew more about the situation than he should have from our brief conversations. Sam did not appear happy with what he was reading.

When Sam finished reading the email, I asked him, "Why didn't she offer me anything of value in return?"

Sam responded with the first of several prepared-sounding lines, "Pay up and we'll talk!"

I was confused, because it was an accurate summary of Jill's email, but not much of a defense in my opinion. It was also delivered in an antagonizing way. I think Sam wanted me to get upset, so he could take control of the conversation and put me on defense by telling me about a law I already knew. Instead, I just sat there straight-faced and didn't say a thing, which seemed to bother Sam quite a bit.

Sam then said, "You do have a defense, [pause] because of the moratorium."

I think Sam wanted me to ask if I had a defense without the moratorium because he threw out the exact same line later in our conversation. I did not comply because I thought one defense was sufficient, and I wasn't there to talk about the defense he told me about the first time we spoke.

Sam then started to tell me what I could do, as if I only had two options available. "You can either file a motion to dismiss, or you can do nothing and it might go away, but…"

This reminded me of Bob's March 19th text message, "you can either buy my house or get out in less than a month." I was there to talk about a third option, so I interrupted Sam.

"I thought that I might have a case against them," I said.

Sam responded with another antagonizing line, "What, you're going to sue the guy over a couple of text messages?"

Bob's text messages had caused me a lot of emotional distress, which I thought may have cost me my dream job. However, I was meeting with Sam primarily because of the clear-cut violations of CT's eviction moratorium. I think Sam was steering me away from a lawsuit against his attorney friend and towards Bob the bully instead. I obliged, because I wanted to hear Sam's defense of Bob's actions before his attorney stepped in.

I had thought that Bob's March 19th text message was legally questionable because my landlord friend told me he was supposed to give me until at least April 30th to move out, instead of April 15th. So, I started down the road that Sam led me.

**Me**: "Well, you start with an illegal text message."

**Sam**: "It's not illegal!"

**Me**: "I thought he should have said April 30th instead of the 15th."

**Sam**: "You can ask them to move out whenever you want."

**Me**: "I thought you had to give them until at least the end of the next month."

**Sam**, after a pause: "An email doesn't count as a legal notice to quit."

Sam seemed surprised that I was trying to make a legal argument based on an actual law, and equally surprised when I accepted his last statement. Just then, I understood what an attorney friend had told me a while back, "I do not think a text message satisfies the notice requirements for termination of month-to-month tenancy." So, from a legal standpoint, you can ask a tenant to move out whenever you want in a text message, though there wasn't much "ask" about Bob's March 19th message.

We then talked about Bob's threatening May 4th text message as well as other ways that Bob caused me a lot of trouble by acting like an unreasonable jerk. Sam's defense was always, "the law doesn't say that you have to be reasonable," to which I had to agree. I briefly tried to make an emotional argument, as opposed to a legal one. This gave Sam the opportunity to cut me off and assert his legal authority.

**Sam**: "You're here for a *legal* consultation, and in my *legal* opinion, you don't have a case against him."
**Me**: "Okay."

I was respectful of Sam's opinion and think he believed it regarding the events we had discussed so far. Sam liked to stress the word *legal*, and I didn't make any other emotional arguments after he scored this one victory during our meeting.

I moved onto Jill's email, though I wasn't expecting Sam to admit there was anything wrong with it after his "pay up and we'll talk" line. To my surprise, Sam volunteered another defense to Jill's email, which gave me an opportunity to even the score.

**Sam**: "Pay them this amount, and they'll drop the eviction and negotiate a move out date."
**Me**: "What is there to negotiate? I am moving out as quickly as possible."

That line worked well because I said the same thing in my email to Jill. Sam's new defense also pointed out the biggest problem with Jill's response: they did not explicitly offer to drop the *illegal* eviction lawsuit. When I first read her email, I interpreted it the same way as my landlord friend: they wanted me to pay them money, and only then would they negotiate the eviction.

At another point during our meeting, Sam tried another one of his lines that seemingly came out nowhere.

**Sam:** "He told you to move out by the end of April, and you didn't do it!"

**Me** (silently thinking): Where did that come from? Am I supposed to disagree with that true statement? I already figured out that you're trying to piss me off and then tell me about some law I already know. You can stop trying now, or not, because I'm happy to keep seeing the look on your face when you fail.

While Sam's lines continued to flop, I used a prepared line to score another little point before moving on to the big question.

**Me:** "Why couldn't he just talk to me like a normal person and we could work something out, instead of making stuff up and threatening and suing me?"

**Sam:** "They're not suing you!"

**Me** (while pointing): "This piece of paper right here states that I am being sued."

**Sam:** "Uh, you're being sued for possession."

**Me** (silently thinking): Well, I'm being sued for something, and thank you for falling for my trap.

Of course, I was pointing to this piece of paper:

| First defendant | Name: | **Osborne, George Douglas** |
|---|---|---|
| | Address: | ███████████████████ |
| Additional defendant | Name: | |
| | Address: | |
| Additional defendant | Name: | |
| | Address: | |
| Additional defendant | Name: | |
| | Address: | |

## Notice to each defendant

**1. You are being sued** for possession of the premises you occupy.

2. This paper is a summons in a summary process (eviction) action

Proof that I was being sued.

By this point, I had gotten about everything I could from Sam, except for his opinion about the violations of CT's eviction moratorium. So, I transitioned to that topic, while briefly letting Sam think that he had successfully defended Bob and Jill.

**Me**: "Yeah, I didn't really think I had anything on them, until this."
**Sam**: "Uh... what do you mean by this?"

I felt really bad for Sam because his heart jumped out of his chest when I said, "until this." I then proceeded to ask Sam the only question I felt I could about Jill's mistakes.

**Me**: "Do you think that this attorney really should have known better?"
**Sam**: "I know Jill well, and she's a good attorney, but she doesn't know that much about the law."

Sam likely had a story prepared to demonstrate how Jill could be a good attorney without knowing much about the law. He seemed disappointed when I wasn't interested. Instead, I just asked him the same question in clearer language.

**Me**: "Do you think she knew that she wasn't supposed to be signing her name on these papers?"
**Sam**: "I've known Jill for years, and in my opinion, she was ignorant of the law."
**Me**: "Alright, then let's just finish this motion to dismiss."

I didn't feel it was ethical to ask Sam any other questions about Jill's mistakes (e.g., "is ignorance of the law a foolproof defense for an attorney?"), because it would have forced him to either give up his friend or give me bad legal advice.

Previously during our meeting, Sam had kept trying to put me back on defense and talk about my motion to dismiss. But I kept control of the conversation, and I wasn't going to let Sam off the hook until I asked him the big question. Sam seemed enormously relieved when I acted like I accepted his answer and finally went in the direction he wanted me to go, which was back on defense and then out the door. I think it is extremely unlikely that Jill, an eviction attorney, was not aware of the highly publicized and controversial eviction moratorium.

Sam then told me that my motion to dismiss was mostly fine, but that he had a few things to add after my first sentence. He then wrote those down for me.

Sam's hand-written additions to my motion to dismiss.

I think this additional lawyer-speak was completely unnecessary, but Sam wanted me to believe he helped me with something during our consultation. In fact, the entire motion to dismiss wasn't necessary, because I found out that a judgment of dismissal was issued on June 28th, the day before I met Sam.

Sam was much friendlier after we finished the motion to dismiss. I was also putting on a bit of a nice guy act while we were wrapping things up. I expressed sympathy towards landlords who wanted to sell their houses while the market was up, and I showed excitement about putting this ordeal behind me and moving to my first house. Even then, I noticed Sam would get nervous when I took the conversation in certain directions, but I just filed those moments in my head for later analysis and quickly changed topics.

The last of these moments occurred when I was just getting ready to walk out the door. Sam started saying, "Let me know if you need any more help", but he just kind of trailed off without finishing the sentence. I knew exactly what he was thinking: "Please God, let this be the last time I talk to this guy."

I felt bad for Sam because he was clearly suffering, and I put him into an impossible situation. While it was ethically questionable to avoid pointing out the obvious lawsuit I had against Bob and Jill during a legal consultation, Sam felt like he gave up his friend. I don't blame him for trying to protect her, and his efforts made me feel more sympathetic towards Jill.

I can even forgive Sam's numerous attempts to agitate me because he was just trying his best to protect Jill. I thought of these attempts as "bully tactics," because bullies love to see their targets get upset. But after dealing with Bob for over two years, I had taught myself how to defeat the bully: no matter what they do, don't get pissed off because you're giving them exactly what they want.

After all of Bob's threats, Jill's attempt to cash in on what was perceived as a successful intimidation tactic, and then Sam's efforts to bully me away from a lawsuit against them, I had somehow managed to make the bullies afraid of me: a software engineer on disability, diagnosed with autism, ADHD, anxiety and depression.

# Can I Walk Through Walls?

I went home and finished my motion to dismiss after my meeting with Sam on June 29th. I used Sam's suggested revision, but I added a single sentence for completeness.

The next day, I brought my motion to dismiss and a required appearance form to the courthouse. I handed these to the clerk, got his approval of my motion to dismiss, and asked him if I could make a copy for myself. He said I could and provided me with two sets of directions to the copy machine. I asked him, "So, if I can walk through walls, I can go this way?" He confirmed, and then I said, "Maybe I should see if I can do that first."

I was feeling pretty confident in my abilities after my meeting with Sam but was disappointed to find out that walking through walls is not one of my superpowers. So, I had to follow the clerk's alternate directions to the copy machine. Oh well, at least here's proof that I filed my own motion to dismiss.

CT's current eviction moratorium. Therefore, the Notice to Quit Possession and the eviction complaint violate the current CT eviction moratorium and this case should be dismissed.

George Douglas Osborne
STATE OF CONNECTICUT
THE DEFEN█
JUDICIAL DISTRICT OF
2021 JUN 30 PM 2 25
SUPERIOR COURT
OFFICE OF THE CLERK

The motion to dismiss that I filed on 6/30/21.

35

I was also required to send copies to Jill. So, I sent Jill a second email after I got home from the courthouse. It was a lot shorter than my first, but much more satisfying to send.

> *Hi Jill: Attached find PDFs of the appearance form and a motion to dismiss that I have filed with the clerk at the courthouse.*

I haven't heard from Jill since her June 23rd response to my first email. I talked to a friend who also knew Bob about the eviction, and I agree with their assessment of Jill's actions:

Jill knew she wasn't supposed to sign her name on the Notice to Quit and Eviction Summons, because they violated CT's eviction moratorium. She advised Bob against taking these actions, but Bob pushed her into doing something she didn't want to do. Jill then completely misread the intended tone of my email and did what she thought was best for her client. If she was going to take the first two steps, she probably felt like she had to take one more when she received my email and thought their intimidation tactic had worked.

I was a little surprised to hear from Sam again on July 8th, when he sent me an email with a two-word message: "Doug, Congratulations." He also attached the following judge's order.

---

The following order is entered in the above matter:

ORDER:
Disposition: JDGDACT - JUDGMENT OF DISMISSAL

The court sua sponte dismisses this action because the Notice to Quit does not comply with the current Executive Orders. See E.O. 10A section 3 which was extended most recently by E.O. 12B.

Judicial Notice (JDNO) was sent regarding this order.

████████

Judge: ██████████
Processed by: ██████████

---

The court sua sponte dismisses this action because the Notice to Quit does not comply with the current Executive Orders.

I thought Sam wanted to make sure I was moving on from the eviction, so I tried to reassure him with my response.

*Hi Sam:*

*Thanks for sharing this, and I really appreciate all of your help. I'm really glad to hear that this case is behind me now, and I'm really looking forward to moving into my first house. I like this place a lot, and even put up a lot of pictures on my website at doug-osborne.com/bear-gulch-rd. The closing process is dragging a bit since the company doing the title work is backed up, but it's still moving along. We've yet to set a closing date, but it should be by the contract date of Jul 30th, and I still should be moving there by the end of July.*

To be honest, I still haven't completely moved on from these events and have yet to decide if I will pursue legal action. While Bob deserves to be taught a lesson, luckily for Jill and Sam, I am not as spiteful as Bob, and I can understand, if not condone, their actions.

Back then, I was excited about pursuing my own "revenge" against Bob, but by far my highest priority was to finish buying my house so I could resume my mission of getting a job and going off disability. Regrettably, my email to Sam only hints at the challenges I faced to become a homeowner that were directly related to the dismissed eviction lawsuit. Fortunately, the eviction also gave me the perfect thing to say to get my house back.

# Part 3

# The House and the Mission

The battle to buy my first house and the continued pursuit of my mission.

# Goddamn Underwriter!

Just before I was served the Eviction Summons on Monday, June 21st, I received the gift funds necessary to get cleared to close for the purchase of my first house. I was still patiently waiting to get cleared to close on June 29th, the day I met with Sam. When I finished my revised motion to dismiss later that day, I felt relieved that this eviction lawsuit was about to be behind me. Just like on June 21st, this sense of relief was short-lived, and a few minutes later I received a phone call from my loan officer, "Greg."

Greg told me, "The underwriter is saying there's a letter from an inspector that says the distance between the well and septic is 65 feet, and that this distance must be at least 75 feet."

I responded, "Wait, I remember that letter, and my inspector said the distance was above the requirement."

Greg reiterated, "Well, the underwriter is saying it has to be at least 75 feet, and that the FHA regulation is actually 100 feet, but some localities allow for shorter distances."

I responded, "Why is this coming up now?"

I thought this was a fair question, because: I received that letter a month ago on May 30th, the house passed an FHA inspection on June 8th, and I signed a loan commitment letter a week later, on June 15th. My closing attorney told me that this type of issue almost always comes up before the loan commitment. Greg, however, was silent after I asked him this question.

I then asked another question, "What, am I really going to lose my house over 10 feet?"

Again, Greg was silent, which caused me to lose my temper and say something that I instantly regretted. "I'm being ****ing evicted! Does the FHA want me to be homeless?"

After a brief silence, as if he was thinking about how to react to the news I just gave him, Greg yelled, **"Goddamn underwriter!"**

A few thoughts were going through my head when I heard this: "What did I just tell my loan officer?", "I really am going to lose my house?", and "that sounded weird." Focusing on the last thought, I was not very convinced that Greg was truly upset at his underwriter. Greg then started to go down a shady road.

Greg said, "Maybe there isn't a problem with the distance. Maybe it's just a typo and the inspector meant to put something else." The way he said this strongly suggested that the solution to the problem was to fudge a number.

I didn't really care much about that number, so I played along and said, "Uh, yeah, yeah, I'm sure that's it, he probably meant to say like 95 feet or something."

Greg went silent again, which made me uneasy, and made me think that he didn't really believe that changing the number was a solution to the problem. I'm still not sure why Greg went down this road, but I thought he might have been evaluating my integrity. I was also thinking that while I didn't care much about that distance, I didn't want to ask my inspector to lie, especially if Greg wasn't playing along anymore.

So, I asked, "What if there isn't a typo? Is there any other way around this?"

Greg responded, "Yes, well it starts with a clean water test."

That made me feel better, because I got to say, "Well, I already have a clean water test that I can send you."

Greg then said, "Alright, then the next step is to contact your attorney and see if he has a survey of the property."

When I got off the phone, I initially felt somewhat relieved because I had briefly thought that I was losing the house. By the end of the call, it seemed like this well-to-septic thing was a resolvable issue. Then I remembered that I told Greg about the eviction, and thought "what the hell did I do?"

I tried to take solace by telling myself that at least I revealed this huge red flag after, and not before, I received a loan commitment from my lender. I knew there were only a few specific reasons that my lender could legally back out of that commitment, and I was pretty sure that my being evicted wasn't one of them. It also helped that I knew I was getting the eviction lawsuit dismissed.

It was still a dumb thing to say because even if my lender couldn't use the eviction against me, they could look for other reasons to back out of the loan. For example, a measured distance that doesn't meet an FHA regulation and is very hard to do anything about.

I also felt very uneasy about how Greg delivered the bad news. I felt like the call would have gone a lot differently if Greg had told me there was a possible issue, and that this is what you can do about it. Instead, he just told me about the issue and seemed to wait until I became upset and reacted poorly.

Greg didn't volunteer any legitimate steps toward resolving the issue until I asked for them. Even then, he gave me an incomplete set of steps to resolve the issue. According to Greg, the first step was to get a clean water test, which I don't think he knew I already had, and the next step was to look for a survey of the property. But I should have asked Greg, "What are the steps after that?"

# There's No **** In My Water

After my phone call with Greg on June 29th, I did some research on the FHA regulations about the distance between the well and the septic. I found that the FHA has regulations for the distance between the well and two parts of the septic system: the septic **tank**, with a minimum distance of 50 feet from the well, and the septic **field,** with a minimum distance of 100 feet, which could be reduced to 75 feet if allowed by the local authority.

I looked at the letter from my inspector and noticed he did not specify which part of the septic system his measured distance of 65 feet referred to. I then emailed my inspector and asked him to clarify. Here is his response.

> *I was referring to the location of the tank. Without a septic contractor digging things up its impossible to accurately locate the septic field.*

I was thrilled when I got this email. This meant there was no problem with any measured distance because 65 feet easily met the FHA's minimum of 50 feet between the well and the septic tank. I forwarded my inspector's email to everyone on my loan team, and then responded to his email.

> *Okay that's what I thought and the situation is resolved now. thanks again for your help.*

My lender had yet to respond to the forwarded email by the morning of Thursday, July 1st. So, I called Greg to verify the situation was actually resolved.

**Me**: "Hi Greg, I'm just calling to make sure you got my inspector's email and that the issue with the well and the septic is resolved."

**Greg**: "Huh? What do you mean by resolved?"

**Me**: "I forwarded an email from my inspector, who said that he measured the distance between the well and the septic *tank*, which is well above the FHA regulation of 50 feet. The 75 or 100 feet refers to the septic *field*, which he couldn't locate."

**Greg**: "You're still going to need to get another measurement."

**Me**: "Why? I have a super clean water test, so there's literally no **** from the septic getting into my water, and there's no problem with any measured distance."

**Greg**: "Well, I think the underwriter will still want a measurement, but you can start by getting a revised letter from your inspector."

While I was a little suspicious that Greg might not want to loan to me after his June 29th call, now I was very suspicious that he did not want to see this issue resolved. Nevertheless, I was going to try to resolve it. So, I emailed my inspector and he sent me a revised letter, which stated the following.

*The distance between the well head and the septic tank, which is a known location, was measured at 65 feet. Distance to the septic field cannot be accurately measured without excavation of the distribution box which I do not do. Given the lay of the land the septic field is certainly farther away but the exact distance is unknown to me at this time.*

My inspector also told me, "If the bank takes a hard line you may need to get a septic contractor out there to dig up the distribution box and measure it." Based on my last conversation with Greg, it certainly felt like the bank was taking a hard line. I suspected this had to do with a certain piece of information that I stupidly revealed to Greg.

I emailed the revised letter to my lender on Friday, July 2nd. I also tried to explain the difference between the septic tank and the septic field, and my email included a diagram of a property with a well and a septic tank. I concluded my email with:

> *I've looked at a lot of other diagrams and in each one, it looks like the septic field is a lot more than 10 feet further away from the well than the septic tank is. I think it can be assumed that the septic field is at least 75 feet away from the well head, and the clean water test attached gives no reason to doubt this assumption.*
>
> *I would really appreciate some peace of mind so I can continue with my plans to pack up and prepare to move out this holiday weekend. I believe that this issue is now resolved and that I should be cleared to close.*

Like every other email I sent them about this well-to-septic issue, my lender did not respond.

# MY Signature!?!?

I spoke to my closing attorney after I sent the well-to-septic email on Friday. He informed me that he did not have a survey of the property, and that it would be costly and very time-consuming to get one. This made me feel like my lender would either accept my email as proof that there wasn't a real well-to-septic issue, or the issue would never get resolved.

Based on my communications with my lender, I suspected it was my loan officer, not the "goddamn underwriter," who was taking a hard line that could cause me to lose my house. So, I gave Greg another call at 3:52 PM on Friday, July 2nd.

I first talked about the loan commitment letter I signed on June 15th. I told Greg that I was 100 percent committed to paying off my loan, and that I honor my commitments. I then started talking about how important the house was to me and my family.

Greg cut me off because he didn't want to hear anymore, which at least meant that he had a heart. However, as a loan officer, it is part of Greg's job to ignore that heart if he thinks the borrower is high-risk. And I had given Greg a very good reason to think I was high-risk.

So, Greg interrupted me, "I get it, you really want the house."

I then told Greg, "The reason I'm calling you is that it is your signature on the loan commitment."

Greg responded furiously, "**MY signature**!?!?"

Greg's almost violent reaction scared me and made me think, "whoa, I really hit it a nerve. Is it not your signature?" I mentally compared it to his "goddamn underwriter!" line and thought, "Now I know how you sound when you're really pissed off."

Despite feeling intimidated by Greg's fury, I didn't back down yet and said, "Your phone call on Tuesday caused my mother and me a lot of stress."

Again, Greg reacted with rage, "MY phone call!?!?"

This time, I retreated and said, "sorry, I know it was the underwriter."

I then asked Greg about my email and said I thought it resolved the well-to-septic issue and that I should be cleared to close. He told me he'd send it to the underwriter, but he thought the underwriter would still require a measurement. He also suggested that it was ridiculous to expect anything to happen on a Friday afternoon. I then let him go from this phone call, but we would see about that the following Friday.

I had really made Greg angry by saying "your signature" and "your phone call." That didn't exactly ease my suspicions about Greg's commitment to my loan, but I also didn't think it was a good idea for my loan officer to be mad at me. Thus, I decided to play it safe before heading into the holiday weekend.

I responded to my own well-to-septic email, where I said that I should be cleared to close. I told everyone that it was unrealistic to expect to make progress on this before the weekend. I also sent a text message apologizing to Greg.

```
Hi Greg, I wanted to apologize
because  I  mistakenly  said
that it was your phone call
that caused my mother and I
distress, when it wasn't the
phone call, it was the news
that something might be going
```

> wrong with this house pur-
> chase that we are both very
> excited about. it's not your
> fault for delivering the news
> and I appreciate your help
> with resolving this issue.
> Have a great weekend and I'll
> talk to you next week.

Greg responded immediately.

> All good and no worries i know
> it's stressful for you. Thank
> you and have a great 4th of
> July!

Suffice it to say that I did not have a great Fourth of July week-end. I felt like my dream house was slipping away, and I did not have a backup plan. If I couldn't buy this house after receiving the loan commitment, then I would have lost a lot of money in the ef-fort. I would have likely been forced to rent another small apart-ment, and I was terrified I would become disabled again.

Further, I had lost some of the self-respect that I gained from taking care of the eviction lawsuit, and from my meeting with Sam. By playing it safe and apologizing to Greg, I felt like I was allowing him to bully me away from buying my first house.

# A Sinking Feeling

My memory of the week following the Fourth of July is a bit hazy because I was under enormous pressure. What I remember the most is this sinking feeling of my house slipping further and further away as the week progressed.

During the week, it became clear that my lender would not accept my email, my pristine water test, and my inspector's revised letter as a sufficient resolution to the well-to-septic issue. By the end of the week, it was also clear that my lender had little interest in resolving this issue. I wasn't about to give up on my house so easily though, so I spent much of the week thinking about how I could fight for it.

Having just won a legal battle against my landlord, I considered whether I could get my house back by winning another one against my lender. After doing some research, I felt like I might have a case if I could prove it was my loan officer, and not the underwriter, who was backing out of my lender's loan commitment. However, I wasn't sure I could prove that. Even if I could, I didn't really want to start a potentially drawn-out lawsuit that I might have to win before I could buy my house.

Meanwhile, I kept replaying Friday's phone call with Greg in my head, particularly his extreme reactions to "your signature" and "your phone call." His fury made me think that it wasn't a good thing for a loan officer to sign their name on a loan commitment, and then get caught backing out of that commitment. I was venting on Thursday, July 8th, when I drafted an email to my lender that I never seriously considered sending.

*Hi Everyone:*

*I was called by Greg McGreg, and he told me that he required that the septic is 75 feet from the well, and that the measured distance of 65 feet wasn't enough.*

*The thing is that the inspector meant the septic tank, which has a Fha regulation of just 50 feet, when you assumed he meant the septic field. The inspector has sent a revised letter clarifying.*

*So the wrong number given was his requirement of 75 feet, and not my measurement of 65 feet.*

*Greg McGreg is now responsible for causing my family a lot of distress for giving me a bad number and telling me that I now need to give him another number. Greg McGreg has been disrespectful, deceitful and has shed all responsibility for signing his name on the loan commitment. Therefore I don't think he should be allowed to sign his name on one of those things again.*

I also spoke to friends, my closing attorney, and my mother, to see if anyone would offer advice or more direct help towards resolving the situation with my lender. While I was offered various opinions, no one suggested a direct course of action that I thought would make a difference.

My mother tried to be more optimistic than me and had the idea that the sellers were taking care of the well-to-septic issue. I told her I thought that was extremely unlikely for a few reasons.

1. It's not such an easy issue to resolve, by, say, moving the well or the septic system.
2. No one at my lender suggested that the sellers were doing anything about it, or that it was an issue for them to resolve.

3. I thought it likely the sellers had a backup offer, given their justified skepticism of my FHA loan, the exploding housing market, and because I thought I got a great deal on an attractive vacation home.

My mother also tried to help out by calling my lender. I spoke to her at 11:29 AM on Friday, July 9th. After conveying my increasingly pessimistic outlook, she said she felt differently because she had talked to my lender and was told that "Mitzy is on top of it." I actually thought she was referring to my lender's insurance agent with the same name, until my mother said she meant the seller's agent, "Mitzy."

It did not comfort me that my lender was talking to the seller's agent, while I thought they should have been talking to my agent instead. I seriously doubted Mitzy was on top of anything other than selling the house to someone else. I thought my lender was just telling my mother what she wanted to hear and had herself suggested.

On Friday afternoon, I was thinking about how rough the Fourth of July weekend had been, and how my hopes of becoming a homeowner had dwindled since then. I was dreading the upcoming weekend because I was supposed to be packing up and preparing to move to my house by the end of July. Now there were only three weeks left in the month, and I had yet to make any progress towards getting cleared to close since June 21st, the day I received the gift funds.

# Redemption

It was late afternoon on Friday, July 9th, and I was trying to think of something I could do before the weekend that might improve my prospects of buying my first house. I was about ready to give up when an idea popped into my head around the end of the business day.

Suddenly, I had thought of a way to use the dismissed eviction lawsuit to subtly both threaten and call out Greg for trying to back out of his commitment to my loan. It would also have the benefit of addressing the dumb thing I said that invoked Greg's "goddamn underwriter" line.

My idea was for a text message that I'd send to Greg, which would include an image of the judge's order. I thought my planned message's accusation and threat were cleverly discreet to an outsider. However, I was fairly certain that Greg would decipher it, and thus considered it risky to send.

I had assessed that Greg was backing out of his commitment to my loan, at least in part due to the eviction, but that he did not want to get caught doing so. If I was wrong, then my message would likely just piss him off and hurt my chances of buying my house. I was confident in my assessment, but not everyone I talked to agreed with it. But it was me who had spoken to Greg three times last week, and who heard him yell "goddamn underwriter", "my signature" and "my phone call." I felt like I had to trust my instincts, even if I didn't have enough evidence to prove that I was correct.

While mulling it over, I thought of a second message that could make the first more constructive by essentially making a peace offering.

At 5:07 PM, I gathered the courage to send Greg the first message.

> ```
> Hi Greg:  turns out some at-
> torney signed her name on pa-
> pers she shouldn't have and I
> got this thing dismissed. I
> had just finished writing the
> motion to dismiss that the
> judge agreed with and it also
> made him unhappy with this at-
> torney when you called me that
> day.
> ```

Sixty-four seconds later, I completed the task by sending the second message.

> ```
> thanks again for your help re-
> solving this well to septic
> issue and have a great weekend
> ```

This is what I was really trying to say with these messages.

> ```
> Hi Greg: Yes, your signature,
> and your phone call. By the
> way, I'm not exactly the best
> guy to mess with. But you
> won't have to find out if you
> stop backing out of your
> ```

```
commitment and let me buy my
first house.
```

After sending these messages, I waited anxiously for about ten minutes until I received Greg's response at 5:18 PM.

```
Thanks for the update and you
have a great weekend too!
```

When I read this, it eased my concerns about my messages by seemingly eliminating the worst-case scenario of aggravating Greg. It was still unclear whether Greg had interpreted my hidden message. At this point, I didn't expect to have anything close to a great weekend, but at least I felt like my gamble had improved my outlook.

I also wasn't expecting to hear anything else until Monday, when I was surprised to receive a pair of text messages from my agent at 5:33 PM, fifteen minutes after I heard from Greg.

```
Hi Doug just want to give you
an update. The lender is re-
quiring an additional look
into the septic system. This
is not uncommon on a property
near a body of water. I have
a professional coming in
Tuesday of next week to map
out a diagram. It will be
$100. After we provide this
to your lender we are all set
to schedule a closing date
```

> We've been working on this for
> the last week but have had
> trouble getting in touch with
> your lender, maybe due to the
> holidays etc but we are still
> in motion.

So, the well-to-septic issue could be resolved by a $100 diagram that was ordered in minutes? And apparently, my lender ignored my agent's calls while they were talking to Mitzy, the seller's agent? Later, I spoke to my agent, and she was convinced she was being "boxed out" of another sale in a highly competitive market.

It is difficult to describe what was the most exhilarating feeling I've ever had when I read these messages from my agent. I was just like: "Oh my God, I just got my house back! That got you moving on a Friday after 5, Greg! You don't get to back out of your commitment to me!"

Greg's response at 5:18 PM was the last time I ever heard from him, not counting automated messages. I still keep imagining the look on his face when he read my messages that day.

On Friday evening, July 9th, 2021, I couldn't believe that I got my dream house back by apparently making yet another bully afraid of me. All it took were two text messages, and I moved into my first house exactly one month from that day.

# Home

July 9th, 2021 wasn't quite the end of the stress over buying my first house, though it never approached those levels again. A bit more was relieved the morning of Wednesday, July 14th, when I received the $100 diagram of my property, along with a letter that said:

> *The property does meet all FHA guidelines in regards to well and septic and leach field.*

I'm not sure how the guy located the septic field because my inspector said it would require a lot of digging, but I didn't care.

The closing process continued to drag on for a while afterward, and I occasionally felt paranoid that my lender may have changed their mind about lending to me again. However, anytime I had doubts, my closing attorney would reassure me that the closing was still in motion.

After July 9th, I never voiced any of those doubts to my lender, because I wasn't going to show them any weakness again. I also never spoke to anyone on my loan team, and only responded to a few routine closing-related requests via email. Almost all my doubts were removed at 5:29 PM on Wednesday, July 28th, when I received an automated message from "Greg."

```
Greg McGreg: We're almost
home! Your loan has been is-
sued the CLEAR TO CLOSE which
means you'll be in your dream
```

```
home soon. My team will reach
out for next steps. Please
call me at xxx xxx-xxxx with
any questions.
```

After finally getting cleared to close, we scheduled the closing for August 6th at 4:00 PM. That afternoon, I drove over two hours from Connecticut to Schoharie, NY. We finished up on our end shortly after 5 PM.

I then asked, "do I own it yet?" and was disappointed to find out that we would have to wait for the final sign-off by my lender's attorney. It was then a tense fifteen minutes of standing by, during which I was told stories of waits that extended over a weekend. Fortunately, I didn't have to wait another weekend.

At 5:23 PM on Friday, August 6th, 2021, I was informed that I had officially become a homeowner. I then asked, "shouldn't there be some confetti or something?" There wasn't any confetti, but it was still an amazing feeling when the house that I had fought for so long was finally mine.

At 5:30 PM, I received another automated message from Greg.

```
Greg McGreg: Congratulations
on your new home. I sincerely
thank you for the opportunity
to work with you. If you need
anything, don't hesitate to
text or call me.
```

This was another satisfying moment. I was thinking, "Yeah 'Greg', I'm sure you enjoyed working with me as much as I enjoyed working with you. You tried to stop me, but I defeated you, and now I get to move to my dream house."

I moved into my house on August 9th and was not disappointed. I've enjoyed taking pictures of my house and the surrounding scenery, especially during my first month living by Bear Gulch Lake in Summit, NY.

A view from my lake access on 8/15/21.

My house on 8/24/21.

My office on 8/24/21.

My living area on 4/8/22.

Sunset from my porch on 8/24/21.

Autumn 2022

# Bullies

Speaking of people I defeated along my path towards becoming a homeowner, Bob was the only one who wouldn't accept his defeat. On July 31st, I sent Bob the following text message as a courtesy because I had told him that I should be moving out in July.

> Hi Bob: we are now scheduling the closing date and it looks like I'll be moving out the 2nd week of August.

I hadn't heard indirectly from Bob since June, or directly from him since his threatening text message on May 4th. Then on Monday, August 2nd, I found out that Bob had gone back to being Bob when he replied to my July 31st message.

> Good Morning Doug, Thats good news but, unfortunately we will still be proceeding with the eviction process for lack of payment for May, June, July and now August rent. I am disappointed that you have chosen this route.
>
> If you would like to make restitution for the total amount owed I will advise my

```
attorney.  Let me know your
intentions today
```

I didn't think Bob's message deserved a response, though I wanted to say something like, "How about restitution for your illegal eviction lawsuit that caused me a lot of trouble and nearly cost me my house? Or for your ridiculous demands that might have cost me my dream job?"

I moved out of Bob's house on August 9th, but we couldn't fit everything onto my mover's truck, nor did I have time to finish cleaning his house that day. I took a return trip on Saturday, August 14th. I still wasn't able to clean Bob's property as much as I wanted, so I asked my mother to finish the job. After she was done cleaning on Monday morning, I finally got to send Bob a short, but sweet text message that I had anticipated sending for a long time.

```
Hi Bob: I have moved out and
the keys are under the door-
mat.
```

Five hours later, Bob crossed yet another line with his response.

```
Your mom should be so proud I
think I will call her to come
over and show her how you left
my house
```

That one upset my mother quite a bit, especially considering she had just cleaned Bob's house for him. She wanted to call Bob, but I convinced her to leave it alone.

Bob kept at it in September, first when he tried charging me thousands of dollars for home improvements that he would have done anyway to sell his house. According to Bob, I was somehow responsible for the full cost of replacing his cheap, 30-year-old carpet, for half the cost of replacing his 1980's stove, and for $300 of leaf removal and shrub trimming.

Bob only waited four days after sending me that "bill" to threaten me with two small claims, one for rent and one for his home improvements. While the forms I received looked like the eviction summons and likewise stated, "You are being sued," they also said that they must be served to the defendant before filing with the court. So, unlike the summons, they amounted to nothing more than a threat, because I didn't have to actually do anything about them yet.

Bob didn't take the next step of filing those claims with the court, and I haven't heard from him since September 2021. I found out that he sold his house in October for $359,000, over fifty times what he threatened to sue me for. I don't think that alone would have stopped Bob from pursuing "revenge," but I think he was also told that he had more to lose than to gain from taking me to court.

As for the others who tried to bully me and made it harder for me to buy my house, Greg's July 9th text message was the last I've heard from any of them. I think that Bob, Jill, Sam, and Greg thought they could intimidate me because I'm on disability, but they all underestimated me. Only Bob didn't seem to learn what I taught myself from dealing with them: that I can stand up for myself and even push back when I want to, and that I am actually far from disabled.

# Banner

I've accomplished a lot since I moved to my house in Summit, NY. I've lost 30 pounds and have gotten back into triathlon shape by running and swimming around the lake, and by riding my indoor bike trainer. I fulfilled a commitment I made to a friend by writing the decorative box software featured at doug-osborne.com. I used this software to make my mother a 120-piece painted Christmas Tree Box and my brother a 108-piece wood-stained Sphere Box. I earned the respect of many nice people who now support me on my mission, and I made smaller holiday gifts for as many of my supporters as I could.

Unfortunately, my mission of getting a job and going off disability has taken a whole lot longer than I ever imagined. It hasn't been due to lack of effort, though I briefly doubted myself in the Spring of 2022. I was having trouble keeping on hitting that apply button due to the tremendous pressure of interviewing for jobs that could dramatically improve my life. So I hung my banner last May to ensure that I keep fighting no matter how many times I get knocked down and feel like quitting.

I start every morning by looking at my banner and saying, "not today." But the best part of my day is after I've worked hard on my mission, and then I kick my ass until I finish my workout, and then I get to say it like "**NOT TODAY!!!!**" because I did not quit today! Now I even have a NOT TODAY sign out by my mailbox.

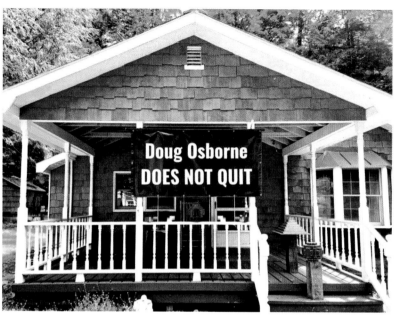

My banner in June 2022.

My NOT TODAY sign in November 2022.

As I'm writing this in March of 2023, I've still yet to complete my mission, even though I've interviewed with some 30 companies since I hung my banner. But like I had to in order to buy my first house, I am not about to quit fighting until I finally succeed.

Because Doug Osborne DOES NOT QUIT.

# About the Author

Doug Osborne is not about to quit fighting today, or tomorrow!

Learn more about the author at doug-osborne.com.

Email the author at DODoesNotQuit@gmail.com.

Made in the USA
Middletown, DE
13 May 2023

30426895R00040